Turn it Off!

Jean Feldman and Holly Karapetkova

Tune: Ain't Gonna Rain No More

www.rourkeclassroom.com

I can turn it off.

I can turn it off.

When I'm not watching the TV,

I can turn it off.

I can turn it off.

I can turn it off.

When there's enough water

in the tub for me,

I can turn it off.

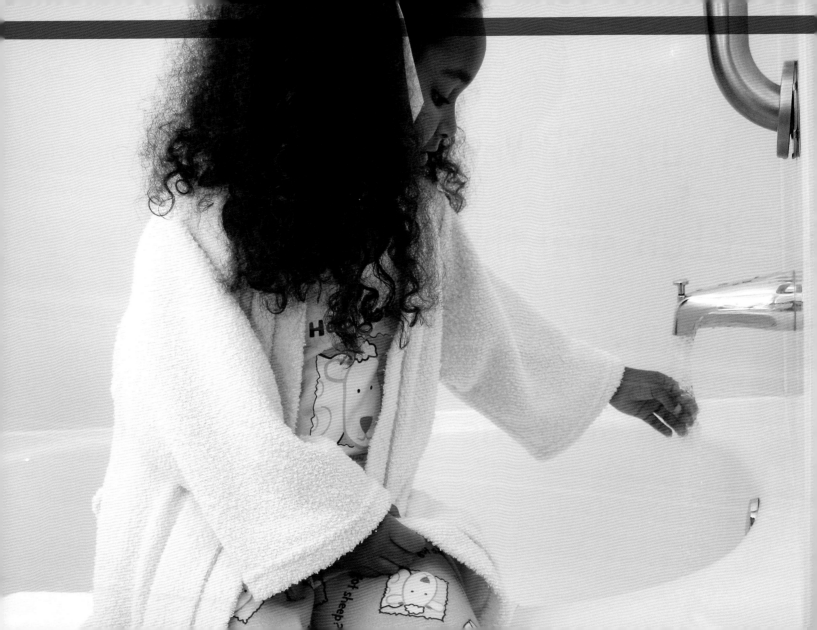

I can shut the door.

I can shut the door.

I can save energy galore,

I can shut the door.

I can turn it off.

I can turn it off.

Batteries, water, or electricity,

I can turn it off.

I can turn it off.

I can turn it off.

If it's something I don't really need,

I can turn it off.

What are some other things that you can turn off to save energy?